THE BATTLE OF
MIDWAY

TURNING THE TIDE OF WORLD WAR II

by Wil Mara

FOCUS READERS

WWW.NORTHSTAREDITIONS.COM

Produced for North Star Editions by Red Line Editorial.

Photographs ©: AP Images, cover, 1, 14–15, 17, 20–21; Red Line Editorial, 5, 19, 29; Frank Scherschel/The LIFE Picture Collection/Getty Images, 6–7; US Navy, 9, 10, 23, 26–27; DeAgostini Picture Library/Getty Images, 13; Universal History Archive/UIG/Getty Images, 25 .

Content Consultant: Dr. Timothy J. Orr, Associate Professor of History, Old Dominion University

ISBN
978-1-63517-021-4 (hardcover)
978-1-63517-077-1 (paperback)
978-1-63517-181-5 (ebook pdf)
978-1-63517-131-0 (hosted ebook)

Library of Congress Control Number: 2016949825

Printed in the United States of America
Mankato, MN
November, 2016

ABOUT THE AUTHOR

Wil Mara is the author of more than 200 books, many of which are educational titles for young readers.

TABLE OF CONTENTS

BATTLE PREVIEW

1931: Japan invades Manchuria, a region of China.

1937: Japan invades the rest of China, starting a war between the two countries.

1939: Nazi Germany invades Poland, and World War II begins in Europe.

1940: Germany, Japan, and Italy sign an agreement and become allies in the war.

1941: Japan attacks the US naval base at Pearl Harbor, Hawaii. The United States declares war on Japan.

June 4–6, 1942: The battle of Midway takes place. The US military, with the aid of decoded Japanese messages, defeats the Japanese forces.

1943: The United States and its allies begin to push Japanese forces back throughout the Pacific.

May 8, 1945: Germany surrenders.

September 1945: After atomic bombs are dropped on two Japanese cities, Japan surrenders. World War II ends.

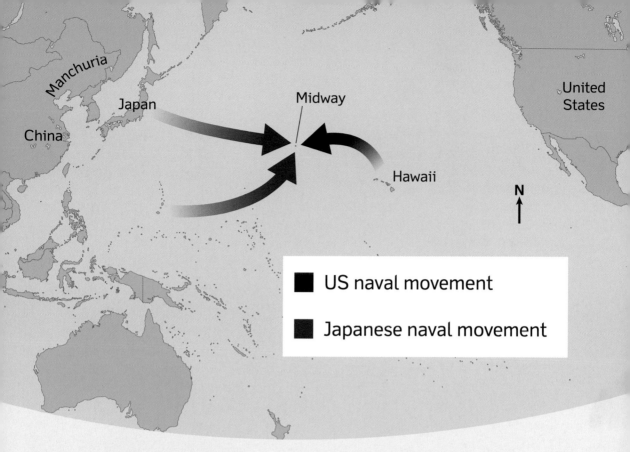

BATTLE OF MIDWAY

	UNITED STATES	JAPAN
Killed	340	3,057
Captured	3	37
Aircraft Lost	145	292
Aircraft Carriers Lost	1	4

CHAPTER 1

AIR ATTACK

On June 4, 1942, a group of 32 US **dive-bombers** zoomed over the open water of the Pacific Ocean. The planes flew in and out of clouds at 20,000 feet (6,000 m). The pilots looked over the sparkling water below, searching for their target: a **fleet** of Japanese **aircraft carriers**.

US dive-bombers patrol over the Pacific Ocean in 1942.

Approximately six months earlier, Japan had attacked the US naval base at Pearl Harbor, Hawaii. This attack drew the United States into World War II (1939–1945). A major part of the war included a fight for control of the Pacific. One important Pacific island was the Midway **Atoll**. This island was the site of a small US military base. Planes and ships could stop at the base to refuel on their way across the ocean.

Early on June 4, Japanese planes had attacked the base at Midway. But unknown to the Japanese, US aircraft carriers were nearby. Several US planes had left the carriers in search of the

The Midway Atoll consists of two islands. One held an airfield (front), and the other contained a military base.

Japanese fleet. One group included 32 dive-bombers, 14 torpedo bombers, and 10 **fighter** planes from the USS *Enterprise*.

Planes line up for takeoff from the USS *Enterprise*.

The pilots' mission was to attack the Japanese fleet before it could send another attack to Midway. At approximately 9:30 a.m., a torpedo bomber pilot saw the Japanese fleet in the distance. The low-flying torpedo bombers and fighters headed toward the Japanese ships. However, the pilots of the high-flying dive-bombers did not realize the other pilots had changed course. The dive-bombers continued on.

The US torpedo bombers and fighters did not fare well. There was a miscommunication, and only the torpedo bombers attacked. By the time the dive-bombers entered the battle at 10:20 a.m., 10 of the 14 torpedo bombers had been shot down. The others were retreating back to the *Enterprise*.

The attack had not succeeded in destroying the carriers. However, the attack did succeed in a different way.

The fight had drawn the Japanese fighter planes to lower altitudes. The airspace was clear for the high-flying US dive-bombers to begin their attack.

The dive-bombers swooped toward the Japanese aircraft carriers. At an altitude of 1,500 feet (450 m), the pilots released their bombs. Then the pilots steered upward to avoid running into the water. Seventeen dive-bombers from another US aircraft carrier also joined the attack.

The bombers focused their attack on the Japanese aircraft carriers. Heavy bombs struck the **flight decks** of the carriers. Flames blossomed outward, destroying dozens of aircraft still onboard. After the battle, three carriers sunk below the waves. A fourth carrier was heavily damaged. Although the battle of Midway continued for two more days, Japanese forces never recovered from this devastating blow.

JAPANESE AIRCRAFT CARRIERS

Japan's Mobile Force was the world's largest aircraft carrier fleet. The *Hiryu* (below) was one of the four Japanese carriers at the battle of Midway.

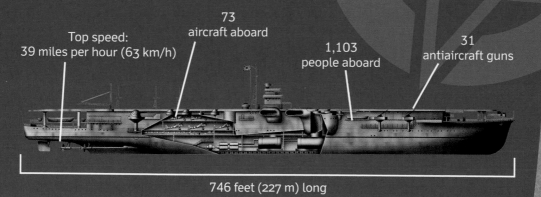

73 aircraft aboard

Top speed: 39 miles per hour (63 km/h)

1,103 people aboard

31 antiaircraft guns

746 feet (227 m) long

CHAPTER 2

A GROWING WAR

In the 1920s, many Japanese leaders were concerned about Western involvement in Asia. These leaders hoped to make Asia more secure by bringing other nations under Japanese rule. In 1931, Japan invaded Manchuria, a region in northern China. In 1937, the Japanese military invaded the rest of China.

Japanese soldiers raise a flag over the captured city of Nanking, China, in 1937.

The invasion began a long war between Japan and China. Many other nations, including the United States, responded by limiting trade with the Japan.

By 1940, Japan was running short on supplies and resources. Japanese leaders decided the country needed to control more land to continue its war with China. They believed their best chance of controlling the Pacific was to eliminate the US forces stationed there.

On December 7, 1941, the Japanese military attacked the US fleet at Pearl Harbor in Hawaii. This attack killed thousands of Americans and caused significant damage to the US Navy.

Sailors watch as a US ship explodes during the Japanese attack on Pearl Harbor.

The United States declared war on Japan the next day. World War II in the Pacific had begun.

After months of naval battles, Japan targeted another US base: Midway. Marshal Admiral Isoroku Yamamoto was responsible for planning the attack.

Yamamoto decided the best way to beat the US military at Midway was to attack with Japan's best ships and planes, and its most skilled seamen and airmen.

Yamamoto believed the United States would counterattack once Japan had control of Midway. Then the Japanese fleet, which greatly outnumbered that of the United States, would be ready to finish off the US fleet.

But Yamamoto did not know that the US military had cracked Japan's communications network. By decoding Japan's secret messages, US military leaders knew where and when the attack would occur. Chester W. Nimitz, commander in chief of the US Pacific Fleet, brought ships to Midway, including three US aircraft carriers. The *Yorktown*, *Enterprise*, and *Hornet* waited 350 miles (560 km) northeast of the atoll.

TASK FORCES 16 AND 17

The US sent two aircraft carrier task forces to protect Midway. The Japanese planned to attack with their aircraft carrier fleet before invading.

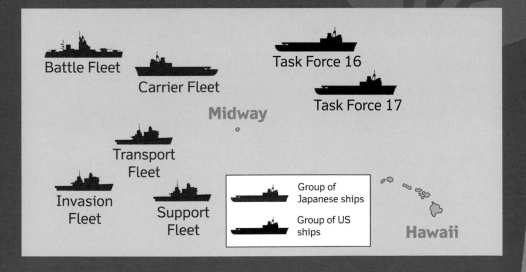

Battle Fleet

Carrier Fleet

Task Force 16

Task Force 17

Midway

Transport Fleet

Invasion Fleet

Support Fleet

Group of Japanese ships

Group of US ships

Hawaii

THREE-DAY BATTLE

The battle of Midway began in the early hours of June 4, 1942. At 4:30 a.m., the Japanese sent 108 planes to attack Midway. Soon after, US scouts reported the attackers approaching Midway, and US fighters launched to protect the base. Japanese bombs began falling on Midway at 6:30 a.m.

Smoke rises from a US oil tank following the Japanese attack on the Midway Atoll.

The attacks resulted in heavy losses in both US personnel and equipment. US fighter planes and antiaircraft guns fought back, but only a small number of Japanese planes were destroyed. Even so, the Japanese attack failed to wipe out the US presence on Midway.

Shortly after 7:00 a.m., the United States launched its counterattack. This greatly surprised the Japanese fleet. The main targets of the attack were the four large Japanese aircraft carriers: *Akagi*, *Hiryu*, *Kaga*, and *Soryu*. Through relentless US bombing, the *Akagi*, *Kaga*, and *Soryu* sank before the end of the day. But the Japanese fought back. Two waves

Smoke spews out of the deck of the *Yorktown* after it was hit by Japanese bombers.

of air attacks sank the *Yorktown*, and its crew abandoned the ship.

The US fleet launched another round of attacks. These attacks focused on the *Hiryu*, which a scout plane had located.

Two dozen dive-bombers attacked the *Hiryu*. The ship was severely damaged. Like the *Yorktown*, the *Hiryu* was abandoned by its crew.

Following the battle on June 4, both sides retreated. Japanese leaders received mixed messages about the strength of the US fleet. At first, Yamamoto planned to restart the attack on Midway early on June 5. However, late on June 4, he reconsidered. The Japanese fleet was still strong, but it lacked the air protection of aircraft carriers. Yamamoto decided to cancel the attack on Midway.

Throughout June 5 and 6, US planes bombed a series of Japanese **cruisers**

US dive-bombers approach the smoking Japanese cruiser *Mikuma* on June 6, 1942.

and **destroyers**. The remaining Japanese fleet withdrew.

CHAPTER 4

TURNING THE TIDE

The battle of Midway was one of the greatest naval victories in US history. The Japanese death toll was 3,057, and the US count was only 340. While the United States lost a carrier, a destroyer, and 145 planes, Japan lost four carriers, a heavy cruiser, and 292 planes.

Antiaircraft bursts fill the air as a torpedo explodes against the USS *Yorktown*.

The battle at Midway reduced Japan's power in the Pacific. It significantly weakened Japan's naval forces and cost the lives of many experienced Japanese personnel. Historians generally agree it was one of the major turning points of World War II.

Following the battle of Midway, the United States went on the offensive in the Pacific. Over the next three years, the United States and its allies pushed through the islands of the Pacific. They gained ground through bloody battles.

World War II in Europe ended on May 8, 1945. But the war in the Pacific continued. On August 6 and 9, the United States dropped **atomic bombs** on the Japanese cities of Hiroshima and Nagasaki. After the attacks, Japan surrendered on multiple fronts, ending in Japan's final surrender on September 2.

BATTLES IN THE PACIFIC

FOCUS ON
THE BATTLE OF MIDWAY

Write your answers on a separate piece of paper.

1. Write a letter to a friend describing what you learned about World War II in the Pacific.

2. Why do you think aircraft carriers were such an important part of the war in the Pacific?

3. What was the name of the US aircraft carrier that was sunk during the battle of Midway?

    A. *Hornet*

    B. *Enterprise*

    C. *Yorktown*

4. Which of the following may have happened if the United States had not decoded Japan's messages?

    A. The United States may not have had time to evacuate Midway.

    B. The United States may have been caught off guard by the attack at Pearl Harbor.

    C. The US base at Midway may have been destroyed.

Answer key on page 32.

GLOSSARY

aircraft carriers
Warships with large, flat decks where aircraft take off and land.

atoll
An island created by a coral reef.

atomic bombs
Powerful weapons that create explosions by splitting atoms.

cruisers
Warships that can move at high speeds.

destroyers
Small, fast warships with relatively small guns.

dive-bombers
Planes that drop bombs while approaching their targets at steep angles.

fighter
A fast airplane that has weapons for attacking enemy aircraft.

fleet
A group of warships under one command.

flight decks
The flat areas on top of aircraft carriers.

TO LEARN MORE

BOOKS

Hutchison, Patricia. *World War II*. Mankato, MN: 12-Story Library, 2016.

Murray, Stuart A. P. *World War II*. New York: Sky Pony, 2015.

Yasuda, Anita. *The 12 Most Amazing American Battles*. North Mankato, MN: 12-Story Library, 2015.

NOTE TO EDUCATORS

Visit **www.focusreaders.com** to find lesson plans, activities, links, and other resources related to this title.

INDEX

Answer Key: 1. Answers will vary; **2.** Answers will vary; **3.** C; **4.** C